A FARM THROUGH TIME

Illustrated by Eric Thomas
Written by Angela Wilkes

A Dorling Kindersley Book

LONDON, NEW YORK, SYDNEY, DELHI,
PARIS, MUNICH, and JOHANNESBURG

Project Editors Selina Wood, Sadie Smith
Project Art Editor Polly Appleton
Senior Editor Marie Greenwood
Publishing Manager Jayne Parsons
Managing Art Editor Jacquie Gulliver
DTP Designers Andrew O'Brien
Jacket Design Dean Price
Production Kate Oliver, Jenny Jacoby

Dorling Kindersley would like to thank:
Martin Redfern and Scarlett O'Hara for editorial assistance, and Peter
Radcliffe, Vicky Wharton, and Julia Harris for additional design work.

First American Edition, 2001

01 02 03 04 05 10 9 8 7 6 5 4 3 2 1

Published in the United States by
DK Publishing, Inc.
95 Madison Avenue
New York, New York 10016

DK Publishing offers special discounts for bulk purchases for sales promotions
or premiums. Specific, large-quantity needs can be met with special editions,
including personalized covers, excerpts of existing guides, and corporate
imprints. For more information, contact Special Markets Department,
DK Publishing, Inc., 95 Madison Avenue, New York, NY 10016
Fax: 800-600-9098.

Library of Congress Cataloging in Publication Data
Wilkes, Angela.
A farm through time/ by Angela Wilkes; illustrated by Eric Thomas.--1st American ed.
p. cm.
ISBN 0-7894-7902-8
1. Family farms--History--Juvenile literature. 2. Farm life--History--Juvenile literature.
[1.Farm life--History.] I. Thomas, Eric, ill.
S519.W53 2001
630'.942--dc21
2001017276

ISBN 0-7894-7902-8

Reproduced by Dot Gradations, Essex, UK.
Printed and bound in Malaysia by Tien Wah.

See our complete
catalogue at

www.dk.com

Contents

Introduction

This is the story of a farm through the ages and of its place in a changing landscape, from the early Middle Ages to the present day. It tells how the farm grows over the centuries from a humble woodland dwelling to a properous house with fine barns and outbuildings set amid rolling fields. It also shows the impact of the farm on the countryside around it, as trees are felled and people work on the land.

The story follows the unchanging rhythm of the seasons, showing different generations of farming families hard at work throughout the year, plowing and sowing, shearing the sheep, harvesting and haymaking. It portrays not only their hard work and craftsmanship, but also the pleasures of life in a close-knit community.

As the story comes to an end, we see how scientific progress leads to an increasing reliance on machinery and how the old way of life, with its traditional crafts and customs, vanishes forever.

Clearing the land, 800

On a fine summer's day, a family of settlers is busy clearing a patch of land to farm. The soil here is rich and fertile, so crops will grow well, and the woodlands will provide plenty of timber for fuel and building. The settlers are renting the land from the local lord of the manor.

The men chop down oak trees and hew them into logs. Oak is the best timber for building because it is very hard and doesn't warp or split easily. The men strip the bark off the oak and pile it into a cart. Later, the bark will be used for tanning animal hides to make them into leather. Nothing ever goes to waste.

The settlers keep sheep, goats, chickens, and pigs, as well as a pair of oxen to do all the heavy work on the farm. They take great care of their animals. The sheep provide wool for clothes and blankets and are fenced in square pens made of wooden hurdles. Every day, the hurdles are moved so the sheep always have fresh grass to graze on.

Beyond the farm, the fields of crops ripen in the sun. There are three big fields around the nearby village. Ever year, two of them are sown with crops, while the third is left to lie fallow. Each field is split into strips. Every household in the village rents strips of land where they can grow their own food in exchange for a share of their crops.

The settlers are building themselves a sturdy house. There will be one big room inside, with space for all the family and a partitioned stall at one end where they can keep the animals in the winter. The walls of the house are made of tightly fitting oak planks; the porch will protect the doorway from the wind and the rain.

The house will have a fire in the middle to heat it and a snug, thatched roof to keep it dry. It will be rather dark and smoky inside, since there are no windows or chimneys, but some smoke from the fire will escape through gaps in the thatch.

Everyone works hard. Some of the men build stacks of leftover timber and burn them slowly to make charcoal. This will be used for fuel, since it is less smoky than new wood. The children's job is to feed the chickens and pigs and milk the goats.

5

Shearing time, 1000

Two hundred years later, the countryside looks much the same, but there are fewer trees. The woods and fields all belong to the lord of the manor, who has been felling trees for timber. The farmhouse has been improved over the years – it now has windows and an upstairs room for storing things. And the farm is bustling with activity. It's late spring and time to shear the sheep, before harvesting starts.

Behind the hurdles, the newly washed sheep are being shorn. The men work swiftly, snipping off the fleece in one piece with sharp hand-shears, while the women tie the fleece into bundles. They will wash the fleece, then comb it carefully with thistle heads to pull the fibers of wool apart.

A neighbor has come to barter baskets of vegetables for some of the farmer's wheat and rye grain. He strings the baskets of grain onto a yoke, or hangs them on his donkey's wooden saddles to carry home.

The farmer's wife spins the wool into coarse thread on a spindle, then weaves the thread into fabric on a big loom. The woolen fabric will make warm clothes and blankets. The girl is winding flax onto a distaff, ready to spin into fine linen thread. Underclothes are often made of linen since it is less scratchy than wool.

Inside the house, a fire burns brightly on the stone hearth. The farmer's wife bakes flat loaves of bread for the family on the hot hearthstones. Meat and thick, filling soups are boiled in the pot hanging over the fire.

Meanwhile, a village wheelwright is making fine new wooden wheels for the farmer's hay wagon. It is a skilled job. He attaches spokes to the hub of each wheel, then drives the curved sections of the rim into place. The wheel rim is very wide and the spokes short, so they won't break as the wagon jolts over bumpy, muddy ground.

One of the farmer's sons jacks up the wagon so that his brother can attach a new wheel. It is vital that the wagon be in good working order by the summer since it will be in constant use at harvest time, bringing hay, barley, and wheat back to the farm. These crops will provide food for the family and the animals throughout the cold winter months.

Hedging and ditching, 1200

Another couple of hundred years have passed, and the old farmhouse is still standing. It looks much the same, but the thatched roof has been extended to make a wagon shed at one end. It is midwinter, and the countryside is slumbering beneath a deep blanket of snow. But the farmer's men are hard at work repairing the hedges and fertilizing the fields in preparation for the spring.

Many of the hawthorn hedges around the fields have been there for hundreds of years, protecting the crops and keeping the sheep and cattle safely enclosed. But every year the hedges are damaged by storms or wayward animals, so they have to be repaired. The workers start by trimming stray side shoots and clearing the ground.

Laying hedges is a skilled job. The workers split the hawthorn stems down the middle and bend them over sideways, to encourage new shoots to grow. They hammer stakes into the ground to support the stems, then weave hazel stems through the hedges to give them a firm edge.

The men are warm despite the bitter cold. Their homespun tunics and leggings are made from coarsely woven wool, held together with leather thongs. They wear stout leather boots and felt hats to keep their heads warm, and around their waists they carry leather flasks of ale for refreshment.

The fields have been plowed to prepare the soil for the spring crops. Plowing airs the soil, breaks down hard clots, and uproots any weeds. Today, the farmer's men are spreading farmyard manure on the freshly plowed soil to make it more fertile so the crops will be healthy and strong.

Every winter, the farm workers clear sticks and other debris out of the deep ditches beside the hedges so that excess water can drain away, preventing the fields from becoming too heavy and wet for crops.

The new house, 1300

*I*t is fall, and the farmer is having a fine new house built next to the well before winter sets in. The old farmhouse will be used as a granary, and a place to store animal feed and tools. In the countryside beyond, most of the woodland has been cut down, but a few mature trees still grow in the hedgerows.

All the building materials for the new house are local, which keeps costs down, and the farmer can afford to pay skilled craftsmen. First, carpenters build the timber frame for the house from oak. It is based on four giant pairs of curved timbers joined together at the top. Each pair of timbers matches because the two pieces are made by splitting a single tree trunk in half.

The carpenters cut the beams for the frame to size with axes and saws. They smooth the beams with a plane and peg them together to form frames called crucks.

The crucks and their crossbeams are assembled on the ground, then the carpenters haul them upright into position with ropes and pulleys. They work on one section of the house at a time, then raise another cruck and start on the next section.

The walls of the new house are made of wattle and daub. Thin pieces of hazel (wattle) are woven in and out of upright oak staves, then both sides are covered with a thick mixture of clay, dung, and chopped straw (daub). Once dry, the walls are painted with a pink limewash to preserve them. When the walls are nearly completed, the thatchers arrive by cart, with long bundles of straw to make the thatched roof.

Thatch makes a snug, waterproof roof, but it needs to be laid on a steeply pitched roof so the rain can run off it easily.

The thatchers start from the eaves of the roof and work up to the ridge laying the bundles of straw in horizontal layers, one upon the other so they overlap tightly, making the roof watertight. They fasten the thatch to the rafters of the roof with spikes of twisted hazel, then tie them down firmly with twine.

The new house will have a big room downstairs, with a partition at one end for the animals. Upstairs, there will be another room where the family sleeps. The floor will be made of beaten earth, with a hearth in the center for the fire, and there will be very little furniture – just a few trestle tables and stools, and straw mattresses to sleep on.

The fields are bare and the leaves are turning. Food for the animals becomes scarce in the fall, so the children go gathering acorns to feed to the pigs. They also collect twigs from the hedgerows for firewood. To the left of the new house, women are thatching the new haystacks. This will keep the crop dry until the barn is ready and the grain can be threshed.

15

Harvest home, 1500

It is 1500, and the farmer now owns his own land. He is properous, so the farm has grown bigger. It is the height of summer and every man, woman, and child in the neighborhood is hard at work under the blazing sun, bringing in the harvest. They must get it under cover before it rains. This is the most important time of year for the farmer, since a successful harvest means enough grain and hay to last through the winter ahead. Every scrap of grassland around the farm is mowed to provide hay for the animals' winter feed.

The reapers move across the field in a row, swinging the sharp metal blades of their scythes in front of them to cut the corn. Behind them come the sheaf makers, who bundle corn into tight sheaves and stack them together to dry in the sun. As soon as the sheaves are ready, they are loaded into a cart and taken to the barn.

Women and children scurry through the sheaves, picking up any leftover corn they can find. A busy family can gather enough corn to make bread for a whole year. They will take it to the miller at the watermill to be ground into flour. Meanwhile, boys set their dogs after fleeing rabbits – rabbit meat for the stewpot is a rare treat.

Farm workers are paid more at harvest-time because they work such long hours. They start before sunrise and continue until nightfall. At midday, they stop for a quick lunch of coarse bread and cheese, washed down with homemade ale.

Farm workers toss the wheat into the barn with pitchforks. Later, they will thresh it to separate the grain from the stalks. The grain will be used to make bread and beer; the straw will provide winter feed for the animals.

The hay carts are pulled to the barn by the farmer's oxen. As soon as they have finished one trip, they are unharnessed, hitched to an empty cart, and taken back to the fields for the next load. The oxen do all the hard work on the farm, pulling plows and harrows as well as carts. They are gentle, but very strong, and are much loved by the family.

When the last sheaf is safely under cover, the farmer will treat his workers to a harvest-home supper. There will be fine food, singing, and dancing to celebrate the end of the harvest. The next day, the cattle will be turned out into the stubble to graze. Then the fields will be plowed for the winter, and the farming year will start all over again.

The new farmhouse, 1700

Two hundred years later, the farm is bigger. The farmer is rich, so he has had a magnificent new house built. It is fall once again, time to gather in the hay, pick the apples, and send the fattened geese and sheep off to market.

The old house has been improved over the years. It now has an enclosed fireplace with a chimney and a new upper floor. This is where the servants sleep.

The new house is built of brick, which is cheaper than timber these days. It has two chimneys, a tiled roof, and stylish glass windows. This means it will be warmer than the old house and will let in more light.

The farmer has replaced his oxen with horses because they are faster. The carter has filled the cart with produce to take to market. Drovers are driving most of the sheep to market too, since there is not enough feed to keep all of them over the winter. The best sheep will be kept back for breeding in the new year.

A farmworker gathers beehives from the orchard, so he can empty out the honeycombs and honey inside. Honey is the main sweetener used in cooking. Before emptying the hives, he carefully moves the bees to new hives. The beehives are made from tough straw ropes coiled into a pot shape and fastened tightly with brambles.

The children watch the pigs feeding happily on farmhouse scraps and windfall apples from the orchard. This will help to fatten them up, ready for slaughtering late in the fall. The pigs will provide enough bacon and ham to feed the farmer's family right through the winter ahead.

Off to market, 1800

It is 1800, and by daybreak the farm is already bustling with activity. There have been changes over the last fifty years or so. The open fields have gone, and the farm is now surrounded with a patchwork of small fields enclosed with hedges. The granary and the old farmhouse are no longer thatched, but have tiled roofs. Thatch is considered a sign of poverty, and the farmer is eager to be a man of progress. It is spring, and the cattle are off to market for the first time this year.

The farmer now grows new crops, such as clover and turnips, in rotation with his grain crops. The new crops make good animal feed, so the farmer can keep more cattle. These provide manure for the fields, which makes the land more fertile, so the farmer can also grow more corn.

The cows are milked twice a day, at dawn and dusk. Milking is cold, uncomfortable work. The milkers perch on low stools which have three legs, to keep them from wobbling on uneven ground. They milk the cows by hand, then hang the wooden pails of foaming milk on shoulder yokes and carry them off to the dairy at the bottom of the new brick barn.

The drovers round up the cows to drive them along the deep green lanes to market. They will take them to whichever market pays the best prices. In the last few years, the farmer has been selecting breeding animals to improve the quality of his stock. This means that his cows are bigger than they used to be and produce more milk.

Like most farmworkers, the drovers don't live on the farm, but come from the nearby village. They don't have any land where they can grow food, so they work for the farmer for a wage. Driving the cattle to market can take many days, so they carry food and clothes with them. As night falls, they usually settle down under a hedge to sleep.

23

The dairy, 1850

Fifty years on, the dairy is one of the busiest places on the farm. The cows provide huge quantities of milk, and since milk doesn't stay fresh for long, most of it is made into butter or cheese. The dairy is in the brick building opposite the farmhouse, beneath the big apple tree. It is a large room with separate areas for butter and cheese making, all closely supervised by the farmer's wife.

A milker and boy bring in fresh milk and eggs. A dairymaid measures out milk for sale. She has left some milk to settle overnight so that she can skim off the cream that has risen to the surface. Meanwhile, her daughter counts out the eggs.

Cream for making butter is poured into a tall barrel called a plunger churn, and plunged up and down for about a half-an-hour until the butter solidifies. It is exhausting work. Then any liquid (buttermilk) is poured off, and the butter is rinsed in cold water.

24

The diary has to be kept spotlessly clean, so there is a stone sink in the alcove, with fresh running water pumped from the well outside. One of the boys is responsible for washing out the wooden pails and cheese molds and for making sure that all the tabletops are constantly scrubbed clean.

Milk for making cheese is left overnight in big copper cheese vats. The milk is heated and rennet is added, to make soft curd. Then the curd is stirred and cut up and heated to separate it from the liquid (whey). Salt is added to the curd, and it is spooned into wooden cheese molds.

The farmer makes a good living from selling milk, butter, and cheese. Villagers no longer keep their own cows, so they have to buy milk to drink. Also, towns are growing fast, and this has created a high demand for dairy products and other foods.

One of the farmer's men takes his gig (cart) around the village, delivering milk. He and his boy load the heavy churns onto the cart. They will take some of them to the newly opened railway station to send to town.

Many villagers come to the dairy to buy their milk. The farmer's wife serves it from her milk pail, using measuring cups. She stirs the milk first, to make sure each customer gets their fair share of the cream.

Next to the table, a girl is cranking a new churn around and around. This churns butter much faster than the old churn. Once the butter is churned, all the liquid is pressed out of it. It is then shaped into rounds and stamped with a patterned wooden mold to show which farm it comes from.

Each cheese mold is in turn put at the bottom of the big cheese press in the corner of the dairy. The heavy weight is screwed down, to press out the remaining whey. The cheese molds are left overnight, then the cheeses are turned in their molds and pressed again.

The cheeses are now firm and have a clean, nutty smell. They are removed from the molds, wrapped tightly in linen bandages, and put on the dairy shelves for storage. The dairymaids will turn them every day for several months until their flavor has matured and they are ready to sell.

Steam power, 1900

Yet another fifty years have passed, and it's harvesttime once more. New sounds ring out through the hazy heat as a steam threshing machine chugs and whirrs in the big wheatfield behind the farmhouse. Life is slowly changing on the farm. Men and horses still work in the fields, but now they often work with machines. The harvest is no longer cut by hand, but by a horse-drawn reaper-binder that cuts the crop and binds it into sheaves at the same time. New inventions do much of the heavy work on the farm, making it quicker and easier. Life has been hard for the farmer in recent years, and machines help him to run the farm more efficiently so he can make enough money to stay in business.

The threshing machine can thresh 25 tons of wheat in a day, whereas in the past it took one man a day to thresh a quarter of a ton. A puffing steam engine drives a system of cog wheels, belts, and pulleys to operate the thresher. One man operates the engine and thresher, while another is kept busy stoking the engine with coal and keeping the boiler filled with water.

Farmworkers feed sheaves of wheat into the thresher. Inside, the grain is separated from the straw and travels to one end of the machine, filling the sacks attached there. One man quickly changes the sacks over as they fill. The straw leaves the other end of the machine and is carried up to the top of a big stack by a moving elevator driven by the threshing machine's pulley system.

Several men are needed to keep the threshing machine working. One wheels coal to the steam engine and another carries water from a barrel on a cart. Others fork the newly cut straw onto the stack. The threshing machine itself is operated by contractors who visit the farm once a year. Boys, who have taken time off school to help with the harvest, chat as they take a rest.

In the past, bringing in the harvest took a whole community many days of hard work. Now it is quicker, and far fewer people are needed. As machines become more common on farms, there is less work for people to do. As a result, many farmworkers are leaving the countryside and going to live in the towns, where there is more work and they can earn higher wages.

Sacks of grain are loaded onto a cart and taken back to the old granary. The farmer sells most of his grain to the local miller, who has contacts with one of the big new bakeries in the city. This is a vital outlet for the farmer since the competition from cheap wheat imports from abroad has put many farms out of business recently.

A wagon piled high with newly cut straw trundles down to the Dutch barn. This new barn has open sides and a roof made of corrugated iron, one of the latest building materials. The barn has a high loading door, so farmworkers can pitch straw from the top of the loaded wagon straight into the barn. The straw will make good bedding for the pigs and cattle during the winter.

The modern farm, 2000

It is a crisp, clear winter's morning in the year 2000, the start of a new millennium. There has been a farm here for 1200 years, although much has changed in that time. The farm now has more outbuildings, and the fields surrounding it are bigger. Many of the old hedgerows have vanished. Gone too are the horses and most of the people who used to work on the farm. These days everything is done by machine. The only signs of activity are workers driving powerful tractors across the fields, preparing the soil for the coming year's crops.

The main farm buildings are still standing. The medieval barn now houses a combine harvester that can cut, collect, and thresh crops all at once. The old dairy has been closed down for reasons of hygiene and has become the milking shed. Even the milking is done by machine nowadays – but the most important machines are the tractors.

Far more powerful than horses, the tractors can do all the heavy work. Two tractors are being worked on the field together. The first one is pulling a plow. The tractor behind is driving a furrow press to smooth out the ground. The harrow at the back breaks down the lumps in the soil, making it fine and crumbly, ready for sowing seeds.

Beyond the big oak tree stands a vast potato drier and storehouse. Potatoes for potato chips are now the farmer's most profitable crop. Here they are washed, dried, and stored at a controlled temperature. They are then loaded onto a truck, for delivery to a factory at a nearby industrial park.

These days, the farm is run strictly as a business, producing more than ever within tight budgets. The farmer works with as little help as possible, so the farm is no longer the hub of a community and most people have moved to the towns. Sadly, the old way of life has vanished forever.

31

Glossary

• *Barter*
To exchange one set of goods for another, instead of using money.

• *Bramble*
The thorny stem of a blackberry bush.

• *Buttermilk*
The liquid that is left over when milk is made into butter.

• *Cheese press*
A machine used to press cheeses, to squeeze out any liquid in them.

• *Churn*
A large can for transporting milk or a container in which milk is beaten to make butter.

• *Contractor*
Someone hired to do a particular job.

• *Cruck*
A pair of curved timbers cut from a tree trunk and joined together at the top to form an upside-down V-shaped frame.

• *Curd*
Soft lumps that form in milk when it is turning sour.

• *Daub*
A thick mixture of clay, dung, and chopped straw used when making walls.

• *Distaff*
A stick around which wool or flax is wound, so it can be spun into yarn.

• *Drover*
Someone who drives a herd or flock of animals along.

• *Eaves*
The overhanging edges of a roof.

• *Flax*
Fibers from the Linum plant family, which are woven into linen cloth.

• *Furrow press*
A tool that smooths out furrows and bumps in soil after it has been plowed.

• *Gig*
An open, two-wheeled cart pulled by a horse or pony.

• *Granary*
A building where grain is stored.

• *Harrow*
A tool that is pulled over the ground to break up lumps in the soil.

• *Hearth*
The floor of a fireplace.

• *Hew*
To cut and shape.

• *Homespun*
Spun and woven at home.

• *Hub*
The central part of a wheel.

• *Hurdle*
A moveable section of fence that looks like a gate without a hinge.

• *Limewash*
Paint that is usually made from a mixture of lime and water.

• *Loom*
A framelike machine for weaving cloth.

• *Mold*
A hollow container in which butter or cheese sets to make a particular shape.

• *Outbuilding*
A building that is separate from the main building.

• *Rafter*
A long sloping piece of wood used to support a roof.

• *Reaper*
A person who cuts ripe corn.

• *Reaper-binder*
A machine that cuts a grain crop and binds it into sheaves.

• *Rennet*
A preparation made from calf's stomach to help curdle milk.

• *Scythe*
A tool with a long curved blade used for cutting corn or grass.

• *Settler*
A person who has come to live in a new country.

• *Sheaf*
A bundle of cornstalks tied together.

• *Shears*
A cutting tool that looks like a large pair of scissors.

• *Spindle*
A thin rod around which wool or flax is wound to spin it into thread.

• *Stave*
A strip of wood.

• *Stock*
Farm animals.

• *Stubble*
The short stalks of corn left in the fields after the crop has been harvested.

• *Tanning*
Turning animal skins into leather.

• *Thong*
A narrow strip of leather.

• *Thresh*
To beat corn so the grain comes away from the husks and stalks.

• *Trestle table*
A table with a horizontal beam on sloping legs.

• *Vat*
A big container for liquids.

• *Warp*
To twist out of shape.

• *Wattle*
Thin sticks woven together.

• *Wheelwright*
A person who makes wooden wheels.

• *Whey*
The liquid that is left when milk separates and forms clots or curds.

• *Yoke*
A shaped piece of wood that fits across a person's shoulders, from which containers are hung and carried.